A Snack for Jack

Mary Elizabeth Salzmann

Consulting Editor, Diane Craig, M.A./Reading Specialist

Published by ABDO Publishing Company, 4940 Viking Drive, Edina, Minnesota 55435.

Printed in the United States.

Credits
Edited by: Pam Price
Curriculum Coordinator: Nancy Tuminelly
Cover and Interior Design and Production: Mighty Media
Photo Credits: AbleStock, Brand X Pictures, Eyewire Images, Photodisc, Wewerka Photography

Library of Congress Cataloging-in-Publication Data

Salzmann, Mary Elizabeth, 1968-
     A snack for Jack / Mary Elizabeth Salzmann.
          p. cm. -- (First rhymes)
     Includes index.
     ISBN 1-59679-527-1 (hardcover)
     ISBN 1-59679-528-X (paperback)
          1. English language--Rhyme--Juvenile literature. I. Title. II. Series.
     PE1517.S3576 2005
     808.1--dc22
                                                                                    2005048807

SandCastle™ books are created by a professional team of educators, reading specialists, and content developers around five essential components that include phonemic awareness, phonics, vocabulary, text comprehension, and fluency. All books are written, reviewed, and leveled for guided reading and early intervention reading, and designed for use in shared, guided, and independent reading and writing activities to support a balanced approach to literacy instruction.

Let Us Know

After reading the book, SandCastle would like you to tell us your stories about reading. What is your favorite page? Was there something hard that you needed help with? Share the ups and downs of learning to read. We want to hear from you! To get posted on the ABDO Publishing Company Web site, send us e-mail at:

sandcastle@abdopub.com

SandCastle Level: Beginning

-ack

rack

sack

shack

snack

tack

See the .

Look at the .

See the .

Look at the .

See the .

The rack has
three hangers.

The sack is brown.

The shack is little.

The snack is good.

The tack is gold.

A Snack for Jack

One day Jack
finds an old shack.

Outside the shack
is a big tack.

The big tack
outside the shack
holds up a rack.

From the rack
on the tack
outside the shack
hangs a brown sack.

In the sack
hanging from the rack
on the tack
outside the shack
is a snack for Jack!

About SandCastle™

A professional team of educators, reading specialists, and content developers created the SandCastle™ series to support young readers as they develop reading skills and strategies and increase their general knowledge. The SandCastle™ series has four levels that correspond to early literacy development in young children. The levels are provided to help teachers and parents select the appropriate books for young readers.

Emerging Readers
(no flags)

Beginning Readers
(1 flag)

Transitional Readers
(2 flags)

Fluent Readers
(3 flags)

These levels are meant only as a guide. All levels are subject to change.

To see a complete list of SandCastle™ books and other nonfiction titles from ABDO Publishing Company, visit **www.abdopub.com** or contact us at:

4940 Viking Drive, Edina, Minnesota 55435 • 1-800-800-1312 • fax: 1-952-831-1632